LOSE YOUR BELLY DIET COOKBOOK:

The Ultimate Secret to Losing Belly Fat, Improve Your Gut and Live Healthy.

By

Brain Thompson

Copyright © 2019, By: *Brain Thompson*

ISBN-13: 978-1-950772-32-2
ISBN-10: 1-950772-32-2

All Rights Reserved. No part of this publication may be reproduced in any form or by any means, including scanning, photocopying, or otherwise without prior written permission of the copyright holder.

Disclaimer:

The information provided in this book is designed to provide helpful information on the subjects discussed. The publisher and author are not responsible for any specific health or allergy needs that may require medical supervision and are not liable for any damages or negative consequences from any treatment, action, application or preparation, to any person reading or following the information in this book.

Table of Contents

INTRODUCTION: 5
  The Ultimate Secret to Losing Belly Fat 5
    How to Lose Weight in This Diet: For Busy People 6

The Lose Your Belly Diet Recipes 14
  Blueberry Oatmeal 15
    Serves: Makes One Bowl 15
  Delicious Fruit Crumble 17
  Delicious Peanut Butter Oatmeal 19
  Red Apple Chips 21
  Savoring Sautéed Kale 23
  Scrambled eggs with Walnuts 25
  Tasty Grilled Chicken 26
  Crunchy Red Apple Butter 28
  Almond Meal 30
  Zero Belly Carrots Recipes 31
  Ultimate Red Apple Meal 32
  World Best Walnut Salad 34
  Crunchy Spinach 36
  Chicken Breast with Eggs 37
  Mushroom Stir-Fry with Delicious Shrimp 39
  Zero Belly Raisin Oatmeal 41
  Vegetable Wrap-ups and Scrambled Egg 43
  Broccoli Vinaigrette 45
  Flavorful Apple Stew and Autumn Chicken 46
  Zero Belly Soup 48

Best Zero Belly Diet Smoothies 50
  Green Tea Smoothie with Berries 51

Black Cherry Delight 53
 Choco Mint Dream 54
 Fat Shredding Green Tea Smoothie 55
 Cinnamon & Red Apple Crumble 57
 Almond Milk Sunrise 58
 Signature Smoothie 59
 Chocolate Peanut Belly flattening Smoothie 60
 Fiery Chocolate Goodness 61
 Zero Belly Cocoa Nutter Butter 62
 Peanut Butter Apple 63
 Best Apple Smoothie Recipes 64
Bonus Recipes 66
 Cinnamon and Apple Oatmeal 67
 Quick & Easy Chicken Salad Sandwich 69
 Tasty Turkey and Cheddar Quiche 71
 Egg Tortilla & Smoked Salmon 73
Enjoy 75

INTRODUCTION:
The Ultimate Secret to Losing Belly Fat

Do you want to be healthy? Do you want to be lean? And finally do you want to lose that annoying fat around your bellies!

The recipes in this book is built around a very clear, research-based concept: it enriched with recipes that nourishes and protects the microbes in your gut paves the way for weight loss, a slimmer middle, and better overall health.

However, research has shown that everyone has some belly fat, even people who have flat abs. That's normal. Remember some of your fat is right under your skin while others are deeper inside, around your heart, lungs, liver, and other organs.

It's not just about losing belly fat. If you have a great gut health it is linked to good health throughout your body. Day by day scientists in this rapidly growing field are finding the link between gut microbes and the immune system, gastrointestinal health, allergies, weight loss, asthma, and even cancer. With every study, scientists become more convinced that having a healthy gut leads to having a healthy body.

This book is aimed at improving your own gut health, starting with the food you eat. In this book much consideration is placed on the diet recommendations, meal plans, and recipes that will help feed and protect your gut microbes. Also, it looks at the *many* other steps you can take to support your beneficial bacteria, from avoiding unnecessary antibiotics to changing the way you think about dirt and germs.

This cookbook covers all the bases, giving you everything you need to know to make dramatic changes in your GI health, your belly fat, your weight, and your overall health.

How to Lose Weight in This Diet: For Busy People

This particular diet also proves beneficial to those of us who just can't always find the time in our hectic lives to run to the gym to do a full work-out or sometimes time to work-out at all. This diet helps you by adding short yet very beneficial and convenient exercises that you can do in the comfort of your own home. Instead of being the regulated sit-ups or push-ups, it gives you exercises that don't just kill you or put you out from the strain on your arms and back.

They're so simple you can squeeze them in before your daily meals without having to completely rearrange your lifestyle. This diet also makes you rethink all the different things you may have already added to your daily routine thinking they would be helpful such as supplements. Many people feel increased levels with B vitamins, since they do state to increase your energy and metabolism, are a great additive to your diet, but unfortunately that's not exactly true.

Due to those who feel the need to overtake these vitamins it actually ends up triggering your fat genes, which you don't want. Your best option here is to stick with the lose your belly foods and if needed <u>one</u> daily vitamin can be fine.

Another downside to most diets is they usually tell you to cut out all sweets, well not this one. It has been proven that the antioxidants in Cocoa can actually help prevent you from gaining excess weight and also lower your blood sugar levels. So with this you can actually eat the dark chocolate you love and adding berries to it makes it even more beneficial. It has also been proven that when ingesting these chocolates, the microbes in our stomach ferment it into heart-healthy, anti-inflammatory compounds that knock out and close down genes linked in insulin resistance and inflammation.

For those of you who enjoy eating seafood there is something you should be sure of before buying your next salmon. The salmon we can buy at the market, although convenient, isn't the best for you as it is full of much more Omega-6s than what you need. So next time you decide to buy your fish instead of store bought go with fresh water instead of farmed.

Also as I stated before peanuts are a great attribute to a healthy lifestyle and diet, and if you like peanut butter that's even better. But, be careful when purchasing your product, if you notice a grocery list of ingredients you can't even begin to pronounce put it back and go with the brand with the most basic ingredients such as just peanuts and salt. All of these extras added in the mix can actually add to those belly fat issues.

Also another food that is more commonly suggested in all diets, a salad, can be one of the most beneficial keys to your weight-loss goals. The leafy greens are great for filling you up without causing you to expand. Adding a salad to every meal can help decrease the extra food consumption and make you feel much better being full yet not bloated. Also just adding a teaspoon of vinaigrette to your salad will prove helpful for your body to absorb the fat-soluble nutrients.

The goal of this diet is to simply remove the visceral fat from your stomach area. So many of us try all of these over-the-counter diet pills, drinks, shakes, vitamins, and even spend hundreds of dollars on those videos that guarantee fast, extreme results of which we can't seem to accomplish and we give up on them quite soon after starting. With this diet you can truly have it fit your lifestyle and preferences and see real, great results much sooner that the others. You can most definitely count on real, visible results with this diet plan, which will also keep you wanting to move up and on with it instead of just giving up on it. This new diet truly gives you freedom in your choosing of foods and how you want to start and continue with it. Not many diets today can say that they do that at all. Also this diet can suit all people of all sizes. You do not have to worry about having the right equipment for a workout video or whether your body can handle doing the things the videos expect you to do.

Also you do not have to worry over spending many hundreds of dollars on all these different pills to help you alongside of having to add the grueling physical activity to those pills to even get the slightest results. The Lose Your Belly Diet is a great new idea to appeal to all of those who have just reached the point of saying, I give up, and help them realize there is another option to choose from and you are the boss in that diet instead of having the diet to control you. In order for a diet to have positive results you need to be able to have a positive outlook on it as well. With this one you can keep your positive outlook on it as well as see results in a physical and mental way which can improve your way of seeing the benefits of the diet itself. Not many diets at all can offer you those kinds of stats for their results. This one can and will prove that a diet can work for you without you necessarily having to work for it.

So as you start out your new year with that resolution you seem to keep failing at, which is trying to lose that excess weight take a look into the Lose Your Belly Diet, feeling reassured that you not only trim your body down to the more appealing size you want but also upgrading your health from the dismal state it can end up in.

What You Need to Know!

The next secret that is beneficial to this diet is what you choose to have for breakfast, so skip the drive-thru run for that biscuit or the sweet cake you grab with your coffee and instead replace it with something better such as oatmeal. With this you can even add some fruit to help it be more appealing to your tastes. Doing so actually tells your stomach to produce butyrate, which is a fatty acid that helps reduce the fat-causing inflammation throughout your body. It's always been said eating greener is always better but actually choosing red fruit over green in this situation is how you can benefit the most. These red fruits having a higher level of nutrients called flavonoids actually help slow the activeness of fat-storage genes.

One other fruit that shows to be a double hit on killing fat and actually curves your hunger is Avocado. Also the unsaturated fats in this fruit help to prevent the storage of belly fat. Along with the foods there are great smoothies that help along the way and show great results as well. Many of the people have attributed their personal success to the smoothies alone. These smoothies add to the decrease of the bloat of your belly. The valuable proteins you take in on this diet are yet another key to your success.

One of the protein packed foods, eggs, is quite helpful because it is packed with Choline. Choline is also found in lean meats, seafood and collard greens, it helps to go after the genes which make our body store fat around your liver.

As always, water is always a key to helping your body be healthy. But with this system they give you some great ideas to make the water more appealing. Some of the simple additives they suggest are adding lemons, grapefruit, or even oranges to your water and of course doing your best to consume at least eight glasses of this water daily.

The key to using these citrus fruits is that they are rich with the antioxidant DE limonene, which is a powerful compound that is found in the peel that stimulates your livers enzymes and helps to flush your bodies toxins and also keep your bowels regular.

There are so many wonderful attributes to this diet to create success for yourself like the fact you have so many options to choose from instead of being limited and feeling restricted from foods you enjoy. You can enjoy the freedom of creating your own trail mix with great tasting things such as nuts, seeds, unsweetened dried fruit, and even dark chocolate pieces, also, don't forget those peanuts. Peanuts are extremely helpful since they are a key source of both resveratrol and genistein, which happen to be two key nutrients that knock out the actions of your fat-storage genes.

The Lose Your Belly Diet Recipes

In this Plan we have include foods that would help reduces bloating by cutting down on excess salt, dairy and artificial sweeteners, heals your gut by feeding the "good" microbes in your belly, and turbocharges your metabolism with lean protein, healthy fats and quality fiber. **Enjoy this Healthy Meals while you lose Belly Fat Fast...**

Blueberry Oatmeal

If you are looking for the easiest breakfast recipe to make in the morning that will help you get the muscles that you have been dreaming of, this is the recipe for you. Oatmeal is a great way to start the day and if it is a little sweet it may satisfy your sweet tooth. Made with fresh fruit and egg whites, you will get the protein and healthy vitamins that you need.

Serves: Makes One Bowl
Ingredients:

¾ Cup of Oatmeal, Your Choice

½ Scoop of Protein Powder, Chocolate Whey

8 Eggs, Whites Only

2 tsp. of Cocoa Powder, Pure

¼ Cup of Water, Warm

1 Tbsp. of Flaxseed Oil

1 Cup of Blueberries, Frozen

½ tsp of Stevia Sugar

How you make it:

1. Mix all of your ingredients together except for the frozen blueberries. Mix these ingredients in a bowl that is microwave safe.

2. Place your ingredients into your microwave and microwave on the highest setting for 1 ½ minutes. Stir and then microwave again for 2 more minutes on the highest setting.

3. Remove from microwave and stir for at least a minute. Then add in your blueberries and continue mixing until it is thoroughly combined with your oatmeal. Serve immediately.

Delicious Fruit Crumble

Serves 3-4.

Ingredients:

1/2 cup frozen blueberries

1/4 cup prunes or dates

1/2 cup almond flour

1 cup walnuts or pecans

1/2 tsp. cinnamon

Brown sugar

How you make it:

2. Preheat the oven to 350 F. Place your fruit of choice in an oven safe dish of the appropriate size. Puree the prunes or date in a food processor along with the almond flour.
3. Add the whole nuts and cinnamon and pulse briefly to combine. Taste and adjust sweetness with sugar.

4. The mixture should hold together when you squeeze it, but be crumbly if you rub it between your fingers. If it is too dry add, a little splash of juice; if it is too wet, add some more nuts.

5. Press the nut mixture down firmly over the fruit. Place in the oven and bake for 30 minutes.

6. Let cool for 15 minutes before eating. Then refrigerates well for at least one day and reheated for breakfast.

Delicious Peanut Butter Oatmeal

For those who thoroughly enjoy peanut butter, this is a recipe that you are going to love. It is crafted in such a way that you will feel energized the more while burning belly fat and looking healthy.

Serves: Makes 1 Bowl

Ingredients:

1 Cup of Oatmeal, Your Favorite Brand

1 Cup of Milk, Skim

1 tsp. of Cocoa Powder, Pure

½ tsp. of brown Sugar

1 Tbsp. of Peanut Butter, You Favorite Brand

1 Scoop of Protein Powder, Chocolate Whey

How you make it:

1. Mix your oatmeal, cocoa powder, sugar and milk together until all of the ingredients are combined thoroughly, in a small microwave safe bowl.

2. Place this in your microwave and microwave for 1 minute. Stir and then microwave again for another minute or until the mixture is piping hot.

3. Remove from your microwave and allow to cool for 2 to 3 minutes.

4. Last stir in your favorite brand of peanut butter and protein powder until your oatmeal is mixed thoroughly. Serve immediately.

Red Apple Chips

This is the simplest, and best tasting recipe ever, check it out! It is quick and easy to make.

(Serves: As many as you make)

Ingredients:

- 1 Red Apple (as many as you like)
- Cinnamon

How you make it:

Step 1- Slice the apple or apples in to thin slices. Make sure the slices are not too fat or too thin.

Step 2- Remove any seeds and sprinkle a hint of cinnamon on each slice.

Step 3- Heat the oven to 200 degrees (F).

Step 4- Bake for a couple of hours until the slices have curled slightly

Step 5- Crunch them up! -

Savoring Sautéed Kale

Serves 1-2

Ingredients:

1 lb. kale trimmed and chopped

1 Tbsp. olive oil

2 Tbsp. walnuts, lightly toasted

1 large garlic clove, crushed

2 Tbsp. lemon juice

How you make it:

2. Cook the kale in a large pot of boiling water until tender (about 10 minutes); drain well.
3. Coat a large skillet with oil. Sauté garlic over medium heat until just golden (about 3 minutes).
4. Add kale to skillet. Stir in the olive oil, sauté until heated through (about 5 minutes).

5. Stir in pine nuts, remove skillet from heat. Sprinkle kale mixture with lemon juice.

6. Transfer to a shallow serving dish and serve immediately.

Scrambled eggs with Walnuts

Serves 2

Ingredients:

3 eggs

1/2 cup chopped basil

1/3 cup chopped walnuts

Pepper

How you make it:

1. Whisk eggs in a bowl then place in a frying pan on medium heat, stirring continuously.
2. When eggs have almost cooked through, add the basil and continue cooking for another minute, or until eggs are cooked through.
3. Pepper to taste. Remove from heat and stir in walnuts before serving.

Tasty Grilled Chicken

Serves 3-4

Ingredients:

4 lb. Boneless skinless Chicken Breasts

2 tsp. Lime Zest

3/4 cup fresh Lemon Juice

3/4 cup fresh Lime Juice

1 1/2 Tbs. Granulated Sugar

2 tsp. Lemon Zest

2 tsp. Garlic, minced

1/4 tsp. Cayenne Pepper

1/4 cup Olive Oil

How you make it:

1. In a small saucepan, whisk the lemon and lime zests and juices with the sugar, minced garlic, and cayenne pepper.

2. Warm for about 5 minutes, until the sugar is dissolved. Whisk in the oil.

3. Remove from the stove and let the marinade cool.

4. Arrange the chicken breasts in a large dish.

5. Try to set it up so the chicken is in a single layer. Prick the meat in several places with a fork, and pour the marinade over the top.

6. Let the chicken marinate, covered and chilled, for at least 3 hours, turning once. (You may opt to marinate the chicken overnight, if you prefer.)

7. Using tongs, transfer the chicken to an oiled preheated grill.

8. Baste the chicken with the marinade and turn the meat at least 3 times while cooking, basting each time you turn.

9. Grill until chicken is cooked through.

Crunchy Red Apple Butter

Serves 4

Ingredients:

6 Red apples

6 cups apple juice

3 cups sugar

½ teaspoon ground cloves

2 teaspoons cinnamon

1 teaspoon fresh lemon juice

How you make it:

1. Core and thinly slice apples into a large heavy saucepan.

2. Add apple juice and cook until soft, about 30 minutes.

3. Pour Red apples into a large sieve and press until all fruit passes through and leaves skin.

4. Discard skin. Repeat process until all apples are sieved.

5. Return pulp to the heavy saucepan and boil gently, stirring frequently, until thick.

6. Stir in sugar, spices, and lemon juice. Cook, stirring over low heat about 1 hour.

7. Pour into sterilized 1/2 pint jars leaving 1/4-inch headspace; adjust lids and process in a boiling water bath for 10 minutes after water comes to a boil. You can successfully make half this recipe if desired. Make 8 - 1/2 pints.

Almond Meal

Serves 2

Ingredients:

2 lbs. asparagus

2 Tbsp. olive oil

3/4 cup slivered almonds, toasted

1/4 tsp pepper

1 Tbsp. lemon juice

How you make it:

1. Snap off tough ends of asparagus. Cook asparagus in boiling water to cover 3 minutes or until crisp-tender; drain.

2. Plunge asparagus into ice water to stop the cooking process; drain.

3. Add oil to a large skillet over medium heat; add asparagus and sauté 3-5 minutes.

4. Toss asparagus with lemon juice and remaining ingredients.

Zero Belly Carrots Recipes

Serves 4.

Ingredient:

6 med carrots, thinly sliced

6 Tsp orange juice

1 1/2 tsp olive oil

3/4 tsp ground cinnamon

1 tsp freshly ground black pepper

How you make it:

1. Place the carrots and orange juice in a medium saucepan.

2. Cover and cook over medium-low heat for 6 minutes or until the carrots are tender-crisp.

3. Add the oil, cinnamon, and pepper. Cook for 1 minute, stirring to coat.

Ultimate Red Apple Meal

Serves 3-4

Ingredients:

2 ¾ small Red apples

1 cup carrots that is coarsely grated

1 1/2 cups vanilla nonfat Greek yogurt

5 cups green cabbage that is coarsely chopped

1/2 cup raisins

1/2 cup sunflower seeds (toasted, raw unsalted)

1/2 cup chopped fresh dill

5 cups red cabbage that is coarsely chopped

2 tablespoons apple cider vinegar

2 tablespoons Olive oil

How you make it:

1. Combine Red apple, carrots, raisins, sunflower seeds and cabbages in very large bowl.

2. To blend, whisk yogurt, Olive oil, vinegar and dill in medium bowl.

3. To cabbage mixture add dressing and toss to distribute evenly.

4. Add salt and pepper, to season to taste.

Tips: To make this easy for you, you can prepare this meal three hrs. Ahead. After which you cover and refrigerate

World Best Walnut Salad

Serves 2

Ingredients:

1/4 cup olive oil

1 lb. watercress, finely chopped

1/2 cup cooked and finely diced chicken pieces

1/4 cup walnuts, finely chopped

1 large garlic clove

1/4 cup hazelnuts, finely chopped

1/2 tsp. pepper

How you make it:

2. In a heavy 12-inch skillet, heat the olive oil.
3. Cut the garlic in half lengthwise and add it to the oil. Cook for two minutes, stirring constantly.

4. Remove the garlic and discard. Add all the nuts and cook for 5-6 minutes or until they are browned.

5. Add the chicken and pepper. Cook 2-3 minutes.

6. Dry watercress before adding it to the oil.

7. Working fast, toss the watercress into the mixture in the pan, making sure it is well coated and barely heated through. If left too long it loses some of its crispness. Serve immediately.

Crunchy Spinach

Ingredients:

2 eggs

1/2 teaspoon olive oil

2 cups fresh spinach

1 clove garlic, grated

How you make it:

2. Remove stems.
3. Wash the spinach thoroughly in warm salt water. Rinse.
4. Chop coarsely. Cook spinach until it wilts.
5. Beat in garlic and eggs. Heat olive oil, in medium saucepan.
6. Pour in egg mixture. Cook for about two minutes on each side, until egg is firm. Serve.

Chicken Breast with Eggs

Serve 1-2

Ingredients:

2 boneless skinless chicken breasts, sliced into fingers

1 egg, beaten

1/2 tsp. sea salt

1.5 tsp poultry seasoning

1/2 cup almond flour

1 t dry mustard powder

1/4 - 1/3 cup olive or coconut oil for frying

How you make it:

1. Heat the oil in a large pan over medium heat.
2. Place the beaten egg in one bowl and the almond flour plus seasonings into another bowl.

3. Dip each chicken breast in egg, then in the almond flour mixture.

4. Cook the chicken in two batches until it is golden on each side.

Mushroom Stir-Fry with Delicious Shrimp

Servings: 4

Ingredients:

2 cups sliced mushrooms

1 teaspoon sesame oil

1 teaspoon olive oil

1 clove garlic, grated

1/2 teaspoon grated fresh ginger

1 cup okra

1/2 cup chopped green peppers

2 cups string beans

1/4 teaspoon ground black pepper

2 cups cleaned cooked shrimp

How you make it:

1. Combine and Heat Stir-fry mushrooms, garlic, peppers, and ginger in sesame oil and olive oil until crisp-tender.

2. Meanwhile string beans and steam okra until crisp-tender.

3. Drain, and add to peppers and mushrooms.

4. Stir in shrimp and pepper until just warmed.

5. Serve over a bed of lettuce.

Zero Belly Raisin Oatmeal

With this recipe you will get the chance to enjoy delicious oatmeal that is made in the traditional way. Freshly baked, this dish will leave you feeling incredibly full while helping you to build muscle in the process.

Serves: Makes: 2 Bowls

Ingredients:

1 tsp. of Oil, Vegetable

2 Eggs, Whites Only

2 Tbsp. of Milk, Skim

1/8 tsp. of Salt

½ Cup of Oats, Quick and Cooking Variety

1 Tbsp. of Raisins

1/8 tsp. of Cinnamon, Ground

¼ tsp. of Baking Powder

½ tsp. of Brown Sugar

1 Scoop of Protein Powder, Vanilla or Chocolate Whey

1 Tbsp. of Raisin, Fresh

How you make it:

1. Using a large mixing bowl, take your Brown sugar and oil and whisk together until evenly combined.

2. Then slowly add in your oats, raisins, egg whites, baking powder, protein powder, skim milk and salt. Top with your brown sugar and ground cinnamon. Cover with some plastic wrap and place into your refrigerator. Let it sit overnight.

3. The next day take out your oatmeal and place into a greased baking dish. Preheat your oven to 350 degrees and then bake your oatmeal for about 35 minutes or until the oatmeal is firm. Remove from heat and serve.

Vegetable Wrap-ups and Scrambled Egg

Servings: 8

Ingredients:

1 teaspoon olive oil

2 scallions, chopped

1 tablespoon onion, chopped

1 green pepper, chopped

2 cups sliced mushrooms

8 romaine lettuce leaves

1/2 teaspoon ground black pepper

1 tablespoon taco seasoning mix, dry

4 eggs and 4 egg whites, or 8 eggs

3/4 cup shredded cheddar cheese.

How you make it:

1. Coat a large skillet with olive oil. Sauté green pepper, onion, and mushrooms until tender.

2. Transfer vegetables to small bowl. Stir in scallions. Set aside.

3. On serving plates, sprinkle lettuce evenly with cheese.

4. Beat together eggs and egg whites. Stirring often, until just firm and moist, in same skillet cook eggs.

5. Divide eggs among lettuce leaves.

6. Divide vegetable mixture over eggs.

7. If necessary, roll up the lettuce leaves and secure them with toothpicks. Serve immediately.

Broccoli Vinaigrette

Servings: 6

Ingredients:

2 tablespoons white vinegar

1 1/2 pounds' fresh broccoli

1/2 teaspoon dry mustard

1 teaspoon olive oil

1/4 teaspoon salt

1/4 teaspoon ground black pepper

How you make it:

1. Trim the broccoli leaves and lower stems, after you have washed it.
2. Cut broccoli into spears.
3. Steam until crisp-tender, for about five minutes. Drain.
4. Combine mustard, vinegar, pepper, oil and salt.
5. Drizzle over broccoli. Serve immediately.
6. Also good chilled as cold leftovers.

Flavorful Apple Stew and Autumn Chicken

Serves 4

Ingredients:

3 carrots, peeled, sliced

1 chicken, cut in parts

1/4 cup apple cider vinegar

1/2 tsp nutmeg

6 Red apples, peeled, sliced

6 whole cloves

1 cup shredded cabbage

1/2 tsp salt

1/4 tsp pepper

2 tsp Dijon mustard

1 cup applesauce

1 3/4 cups low sodium chicken broth, warm

How you make it:

1. Heat large Dutch oven over medium high temperature, after spraying with vegetable cooking spray.

2. Add chicken turning to brown on all sides, and cook, about 10 minutes.

3. Sprinkle with nutmeg, pepper and salt.

4. Spread mustard over chicken pieces; add warm broth, cloves, carrots and vinegar; bring to a boil.

5. Reduce heat to low, Cover and cook 15 minutes.

6. Add apples and cook for about five minutes.

7. Add cabbage, stirring into liquid. Cook, covered, until fork can be inserted in chicken with ease, about 10 minutes more.

8. With slotted spoon, remove vegetables and chicken to warm serving bowl and keep warm.

9. Stir applesauce, into liquid; boil on high temperature for about 5 minutes and pour over chicken and vegetables.

10. Serve with brown rice, if desired.

Zero Belly Soup

Servings: 8

Ingredients:

2 quarts' homemade chicken broth

1-pound spinach, thoroughly washed

4 whole eggs

1/4 cup fresh basil leaves

1/4 cup fresh parsley

2 tablespoons lemon juice

1/2 cup freshly grated Parmesan cheese

1/2 teaspoon ground black pepper

How you make it:

1. Boil chicken broth in large pan.
2. Remove stems from spinach.
3. Tear each leaf in quarters.
4. Rinse and set aside.
5. Beat together parsley, basil, lemon juice, eggs, Parmesan and pepper.
6. Set aside. 5 minutes before serving, and working quickly, stir spinach into broth.
7. Cook about a minute longer.
8. Using wire whisk, stir egg mixture into the broth, adding the eggs gradually so they don't clump.
9. This should be wispy looking.
10. Continue to whisk, about 2 minutes until egg is cooked through.
11. Serve immediately.

Best Zero Belly Diet Smoothies

In this plan, we have included The Best, healthy and delicious smoothie recipes. This is an easy way to combine all the foods required in the Zero Belly Diet in a delicious beverage meal in no time. It is quick and easy. Start whizzing your way to a healthier You.

Green Tea Smoothie with Berries

How about stopping for a smoothie which has the best and natural ingredients giving you a power packed nutritional jam session?

Serves 1

Ingredients:

- ¾ cup of Fortified Vanilla Soy Milk (Light and rich in calcium C)
- ½ Banana (medium sized)
- 1 ½ cups of Blueberries (frozen)
- 2 teaspoons of Honey
- 1 Green Tea bag
- 3 tablespoons of Water

How you make it:

Step 1- Place the water in a small bowl and heat in the microwave until it is steaming hot. Add the Green tea bag and let it brew for 3 minutes. After you remove the bag, add the honey and stir until it sets.

Step 2- Take out your blender and blend the milk, banana, and the berries.

Step 3- Add the tea which you made in step 1 to the mixture which you blended in step 2. Blend all of the ingredients once again. If needed, add a bit more water to the mixture.

Step 4- Pour the delicious smoothie out and serve in a tall glass.

Black Cherry Delight

Serves 1

Ingredients:

1 cup almond milk (sometimes a little more)

3 ice cubes

1 Tbs. flaxseed

1/2 cup of frozen black cherries

1 tbs. Cacao

How you make it:

1. Mix the milk and frozen fruit in a blender and then add the rest.
2. Blend until Smooth and Creamy.
3. I use a Vitamix, you can use any blender of your choice. So yummy!

Note: You can Add frozen blueberries too; you would definitely love it!

Choco Mint Dream

serves 1

Ingredients:

1 Frozen Banana

1/4 tsp Peppermint or Mint Flavor Oil

1 Egg Yolk (Optional)

Raw Cacao (Optional)

1 Cup Raw Cow's Milk (Or water)

How you make it:

1. I blend all at once, usually shaking up the liquid and powder first helps prevent it getting stuck to the blender though.
2. Blend till smooth & Creamy. Enjoy!

Fat Shredding Green Tea Smoothie

Yield: Makes 1 Servings

Ingredients:

- 1 cup green tea, chilled
- 1 cup loosely packed cilantro
- ½ avocado
- 1 cup loosely packed organic baby kale (or another baby green)
- 1 cup pineapple
- juice of 1 lemon
- 1 cup cucumber
- 1 tablespoon fresh ginger, grated

How you make it:

- Place all ingredients in a blender, and blend until smooth.
- Serve Immediately

Cinnamon & Red Apple Crumble

Yield: Make 1 Servings

Ingredients:

- 1/2 red apple, peeled & cored
- 1 teaspoon local honey
- 2 tablespoons pecans
- 1 tablespoon flax seed
- 1/2 cup rolled oats
- 1 cup unsweetened vanilla almond milk
- Dash apple pie spice

How you make it:

- Add all ingredients to blender
- Blend on high, adding water and/or ice (if necessary), to reach desired consistency

Almond Milk Sunrise

Yield: Make 1 Servings

Ingredients:

- 2 tablespoons Raw Cacao Powder
- 1 serving chocolate whey protein powder
- 1-2 tablespoons instant coffee
- 1 tablespoon cashews
- 1 cup unsweetened chocolate almond milk
- 1 cup ice

How you make it:

- Mix all ingredients in blender, blend on high until smooth.
- Add water and/or ice to reach desired consistency.

Signature Smoothie

Yield: Makes 1 Serving

Ingredients:

- 1 cup unsweetened vanilla almond milk
- ½ cup of baby kale
- 1 teaspoon cinnamon
- 2 tablespoons lemon juice
- 1 cup cooked, peeled sweet potato
- 1 scoop of Vanilla Protein Powder
- ½ cup crushed ice

How you make it:

- Combine all ingredients to blender
- Blend on high, adding water and/or ice (if necessary), to reach desired consistency

Chocolate Peanut Belly flattening Smoothie

Yield: Make 1 Servings

Ingredients:

- 1 tablespoon natural peanut butter
- 1 serving chocolate whey protein powder
- 1 tablespoon Raw Cacao Powder
- 1/2 frozen banana
- 1 cup unsweetened chocolate almond milk
- 1 cup ice cubes

How you make it:

- Peel banana before placing in the freezer. Freeze overnight.
- Mix all ingredients in blender, blend on high.
- Add water and/or ice (if necessary) to reach desired consistency.

Fiery Chocolate Goodness

Yield: Make 1 Servings

Ingredients:

- 2 tablespoons Raw Cacao Powder
- 2 handfuls fresh spinach
- 1 cup unsweetened chocolate almond milk
- 1 serving chocolate whey protein powder
- 1/4 avocado, peeled and flesh removed
- 1 cup ice cubes
- Dash cinnamon, to taste
- Dash cayenne powder, to taste

How you make it:

- Open avocado, remove seed and scoop out 1/4 with a spoon
- Mix all ingredients in blender, blend on high.
- Add water to reach desired consistency.

Zero Belly Cocoa Nutter Butter

Yield: Make 1 Servings

Ingredients:

- 2 tablespoons Raw Cacao Powder
- 2 large handfuls raw spinach
- 2 tablespoons natural peanut butter
- 1 - 1.5 cups unsweetened vanilla almond milk
- 1/2 frozen banana

How you make it:

- Peel banana before placing in the freezer. Freeze overnight.
- Mix all ingredients in blender, blend on high.
- Add water and/or ice (if necessary) to reach desired consistency.

Peanut Butter Apple

Serves 1

Ingredients:

- 1 red apple, peeled and cored
- 2 tablespoons natural peanut butter
- 1 cup plain Greek yogurt (we use Chobani)
- 1 tablespoon flax seed
- 1 cup unsweetened vanilla almond milk

How you make it:

- Add all ingredients to blender
- Blend on high, adding water and/or ice (if necessary), to reach desired consistency

Best Apple Smoothie Recipes

Apple is a great fruit that taste really well when used in making smoothie. Apple can be some of the healthiest foods to eat. The deeper the color, the more effective they are at helping turn off obesity genes. It has wonderful flavors, which makes drinking smoothies an ultimate delight.

Serves 2

Ingredients:

4 cups of kale

4 small red apples

½ lemon juice

1 cup ice

How you make it:

1. First, Place the kale and water into blender and blend until mixture is a green juice-like consistency.

2. Stop blender and add the other remaining ingredients and blend.

3. Add ice if desired and blend again until creamy.

Bonus Recipes

We have created this recipe to give you lots of delicious variety to choose from while on this Diet Plan... Enjoy!

Cinnamon and Apple Oatmeal

It is no secret that oatmeal is one of the easiest breakfast items to make. With this recipe you can enjoy easy to make oatmeal as well with a touch of the delicious apple flavor most people crave.

Serves 4

Ingredients:

1 ½ Cups of Oats, Cooking and Quick

4 Scoops of Protein Powder, Chocolate Whey

1 Tbsp. of Brown Sugar

1/3 Cup of Dry Milk Powder, Nonfat and Optional

¼ tsp. of Salt

1 Tbsp. of brown Sugar

¾ tsp. of Cinnamon, Ground

¼ Cup of Apples, Dried and Diced Finely

1/8 tsp. of Cloves, Ground

½ Cup of Water Per Serving Made

How you make it:

1. Mix all of your ingredients together except for your water into a small sized mixing bowl.

2. To make oatmeal scoop out ½ Cup of your oatmeal mixture. Store the rest in an air-tight container. In a small saucepan mix together your oatmeal and water and heat up over medium heat. Allow to cook for about 1 minute or longer until it reaches the consistency you desire. Serve while still piping hot and enjoy.

Quick & Easy Chicken Salad Sandwich

This is the perfect recipe to make if you find yourself pressed for time and just want to enjoy something quick. Not only does it taste great, but it will help you burn belly fat and build your muscles in no time.

Makes: 2 Sandwiches

Ingredients:

1 Stick of Celery, Chopped Finely

1 Tbsp. of Pine Nuts

1 Tbsp. of Onion, Chopped Finely

1 tsp. of Sour Cream, Fat Free

1 tsp. of Spicy Mustard, Brown

1 tsp. of Yogurt, Plain and Fat Free

2 Lettuce Leaves

2, 3 Ounce Cans of Chicken, Chunks, Rinsed and Fully Drained at Least Twice

Dash of Pepper for Taste

4 Slices of Bread, Whole Grain

How you make it:

1. In a medium sized mixing bowl combine your sour cream, celery, mustard, pepper, pine nuts and onions together until all of the ingredients are thoroughly mixed together. Mix in your chicken gently.

2. On your slices, spread some of the mixture onto each slice. Top with your lettuce leaves and another slice of bread. Repeat and serve immediately.

Tasty Turkey and Cheddar Quiche

This recipe makes a quiche that you will instantly fall in love with. This quiche recipe allows you to make a dish that is packed full of the nutrients you are looking for to help fuel your fat burning efforts.

Makes: 16 Quiches

Ingredients:

12 Ounces of Turkey, Italian Seasoned Preferable and Chopped Finely

¼ Cup of Spinach, Fresh and Chopped Finely

½ Cup Onions, Chopped Finely

¼ Cup Green Bell Peppers, Chopped Finely

5 Eggs, Large in Size

1 Cup of Egg Whites

¼ Cup of Almond Milk, Unsweetened

1 Cup of Cheddar Cheese, Shredded

¼ tsp. of Black Pepper for Taste

How you make it:

1. Preheat your oven to 350 degrees. While your oven heats up take out a saucepan and heat up 1 Tbsp. of Olive Oil over medium to high heat. Cook your turkey until it is fully browned. Remove from heat.

2. In a medium sized mixing bowl, beat together your eggs, pepper and milk together until everything is thoroughly combined. Then stir in your cooked turkey, vegetables and cheese and mix evenly.

3. Take out a muffin tin and line it with some parchment pepper. Then distribute about ¼ cup of your mix into each of the tins.

4. Place your muffin tin into your oven and allow to bake for 30 minutes or until it is set. Remove from heat and allow the quiches to cool for 5 minutes before you serve.

Egg Tortilla & Smoked Salmon

In the need for a seafood fix? Try this smoking salmon and egg recipe, get it served with delicious tortilla bread. The perfect dish for a party of 2.

Serves: 2

Ingredients:

- Salt and Pepper
- 4 Eggs
- 2 handfuls of Alfalfa Sprouts
- 1 Avocado (sliced)
- 6 slices of Smoked Salmon
- 2 Tortillas (whole-wheat)

How you make it:

Step 1- Toast the Tortilla bread. No toaster? Throw it in the microwave for just 1 minute!

Step 2- Place 3 slices of the Salmon on each of the Tortilla bread.

Step 3- Layer it off with the Avocado slices and Alfalfa sprouts.

Step 4- Fry the eggs; it is better if you keep the yolk at medium. Add salt and pepper for seasoning.

Step 5- Top the dish off with the fried eggs; break the yolk so that it drips down on the rest of the dish. Hot sauce can be added on top as well.

Step 6- Make the most of it!

Enjoy

If you Follow through the ultimate guideline provided in The Lose Your Belly Diet by Travis Stork and Zero Belly Diet By David Zinczenko, And some of the Healthy and Delicious recipes we have worked so hard to make for you. You are going to be seeing great results in your body and health, because it is proven to work.

If you enjoyed the recipes in this book, please take the time to share your thoughts and post a positive review with 5-star rating on Amazon, it would encourage us and make us serve you better. It'll be greatly appreciated!

www.ingramcontent.com/pod-product-compliance
Lightning Source LLC
Chambersburg PA
CBHW081730100526
44591CB00016B/2569